GW01551541

ANTI-INFLAMMATORY DIET FOR BEGINNERS

A COMPLETE PLAN FOR STAYING HEALTHY, EATING WELL, AND HEALING THE IMMUNE SYSTEM

ADAM WEIL

PUBLISHING FORTE

INTRODUCTION

Inflammation is the cause of several ailments, and if it is not properly managed, it can lead to death. There are several treatments given by experts and doctors for inflammation. An anti-inflammatory diet is the best and most effective amongst them. In this book, you will learn everything there is to know about inflammation, the types of diseases it can lead to, their causes, and treatment. You will find the best inflammatory foods and how best to use them in making up your own anti-inflammatory menu.

CHAPTER ONE: THE MEANING OF INFLAMMATION

The body has a defense mechanism that protects it from intrusive occurrences that will deter the good health of any individual. Inflammation is part of the aforementioned defense mechanism that plays a vital role in the body's healing process.

THE BODY LAUNCHES a biological response when an intruder is detected. The biological reaction is meant to eradicate the intruder. The intruder could be an irritant, a thorn, or a pathogen. There are different types of pathogens which include; viruses, bacteria, and many more. These pathogens can cause infections once they gain access to the body.

THE HUMAN BODY is quite unique; at certain times, it accidentally identifies its own tissues and cells as dangerous and reacts to it. Such accidental responses may lead to autoimmune diseases like type I diabetes. According to specialists, the cause of a lot of chronic diseases is inflammation. Some of these

Anti-Inflammatory Diet for Beginners 3

diseases include obesity, type 2 diabetes, and heart disease. Individuals who have the ailments, as mentioned earlier, possess heightened levels of inflammatory markers embedded in them.

Acute Inflammation

There are two types of inflammation which are chronic and acute inflammation. Acute inflammation is the immune system reacting to intruders to the body. It lasts for a short time. Acute inflammation is mostly caused by the presence of harmful pathogens in the body, tissue injury. Treating acute inflammation is quite simple as it is not usually critical. It can be treated with CBD oil (to abate swelling), compression, and rest. Although acute inflammation is beneficial to the overall well-being of a person, its after-effects must be treated to avoid the development of injury or infection that can cause unbearable pain. For instance, if one does not treat a broken bone, the situation can degenerate.

ACUTE INFLAMMATION IS QUITE minor and can be easily treated. The symptoms are quite obvious, which makes it easy to detect.

Chronic Inflammation

Between the previously discussed acute inflammation and chronic inflammation, chronic inflammation is the most dangerous of the two. An individual experiences chronic inflammation when the aforementioned biological response of the body to intruders lingers. The human body is alert at all times. After a long period of reacting, the organs and tissues are negatively affected by inflammation. According to research,

certain conditions like asthma and cancer are also enabled by chronic inflammation.

Symptoms Of Chronic Inflammation

The symptoms of chronic inflammation are quite subtle, which makes it go unnoticeable when it first occurs. Some common causes of inflammation include; fever, mouth sores, fatigue, chest pain, abdominal pain, rashes, etc.

The symptoms mentioned above can be minor or severe. They can linger for several days, months, and years if not promptly attended to.

Causes Of Chronic Inflammation

Chronic inflammation is caused by several things like; injury or infection, over-exposure to irritants (polluted air or chemicals), an autoimmune disorder (the immune system accidentally attacking healthy cells and tissues).

HOWEVER, these causes do not affect everybody as every human body reacts differently to things. Additionally, there are cases of chronic inflammation with no detectable cause. According to experts, chronic inflammation is enabled by a range of factors like; chronic stress, smoking, alcohol, obesity, and many others.

How The Body Is Affected By Chronic Inflammation

As mentioned earlier, healthy organs, tissues, and cells can be damaged by the body's inflammatory response when you go through chronic inflammation. If this continues for a long time, it can cause internal scarring, tissue death, and DNA damage.

All of this can lead to a breakdown of an individual's overall health.

INTERNAL SCARRING, DNA damage, and tissue death all have one thing in common. They all lead to developing many diseases in the body like; type 2 diabetes, cancer, asthma, obesity, rheumatoid arthritis, heart disease, and neurodegenerative ailments like Alzheimer's disease.

Treatment Of Chronic Inflammation

Inflammation occurs when the body tries to heal itself, which makes it a natural occurrence. However, it is imperative to control it when it becomes chronic, which delineates the probability of elongated damage. Below are some methods to treat inflammation:

- **Steroids**

There is a steroid hormone type called corticosteroid. They are utilized to treat chronic inflammation. Corticosteroids suppress the immune system and lessen inflammation. The suppression of the immune system is helpful, especially when the immune system has waged war on healthy tissues and cells. However, using corticosteroids can cause osteoporosis, high blood pressure, and vision problems. During the prescription of this treatment, the risks and benefits are broken down to patients by doctors.

- **NSAIDs (Nonsteroidal Anti-Inflammatory Drugs)**

Some patients may be affected by the side effects of corticosteroids than others. There is a solution for that probability.

Over-the-counter drugs like naproxen, ibuprofen, and aspirin eradicate pain and inflammation effectively. However, using these drugs for too long can cause a high probability of ailments like kidney disease and peptic ulcer disease.

- **Supplements**

Supplements are some of the best solutions for a plethora of health issues. They are effective in the treatment of inflammation. Supplements like; curcumin, fish oil, and lipoic acid abate diseases associated with inflammation.

- **Spices**

Certain spices may aid in the ablation of inflammatory diseases and inflammation. Some of these spices include cayenne, garlic, and ginger.

THE RISK of a plethora of dangerous ailments is heightened by inflammation. Inflammation can be detected by your doctor via blood tests. Supplements, medication, and an *anti-inflammatory diet (explored in chapter five)* can decrease inflammation risk. Maintenance of healthy body weight, staying away from alcohol, and not smoking can reduce inflammation risk.

2

CHAPTER TWO: INFLAMMATION FELT BY THE BODY

The types of inflammation in chapter one (especially chronic inflammation) are felt in different areas of the body. These experiences occur both outside and inside the body. Some of the inflammation felt outside the body and inside (the organs) have been mentioned earlier. In this chapter, inflammation felt inside the body is discussed.

GERD and Inflammation

GERD is an acronym for Gastroesophageal Reflux Disease, and it causes **esophagitis.** Esophagitis is inflammation of the esophagus; for the benefit of those who have no idea what an esophagus is, an esophagus is a tube that links the stomach and throat. In other words, an esophagus is a pipe that transports food from the mouth to the stomach.

Symptoms Of Esophagitis

There are several symptoms of esophagitis in the body; some of them include; acid reflux, cough, abdominal pain, heartburn,

painful swallowing, sore throat, hoarseness, nausea, unpleasant mouth tastes, vomiting, mouth sores, bad breath, indigestion, and chest pain.

Grades Of Esophagitis

Medical practitioners have developed a grading system that helps decipher the severity of esophagitis. The most used classification system is the Los Angeles (LA) classification system.

- **Grade A:** In this grade, one or more mucosal break that is about 5mm long does not surpass two mucosal folds' top.
- **Grade B:** In this grade, one or more mucosal breaks beyond 5mm long do not surpass two mucosal folds' top.
- **Grade C:** In this grade, one or more mucosal breaks persists between two mucosal folds' top. However, this involves just about 30% of the circumference.
- **Grade D:** In this grade, almost 80% of the esophageal circumference partakes in the mucosal break.

The Savary-Miller classification was used by virtually everyone in the past. Still, they turned their attention to the Los Angeles Classification because of how thorough it is instead of the Savary-Miller classification.

Types Of Esophagitis

There are different types of this ailment; let us take a look at some of them.

Anti-Inflammatory Diet for Beginners   9

- **Infectious Esophagitis:** This is the type of esophagitis caused by fungus, bacteria, or viruses
- **Reflux Esophagitis:** This occurs when the stomach acid refluxes into the esophagus.
- **Eosinophilic Esophagitis occurs when there is a heightened number of blood cell types** in the esophageal wall lining. This has been described by experts as an allergic reaction. Eosinophilic esophagitis causes the esophageal muscles to weaken, thereby causing challenges in swallowing meals.
- **Graft-Versus-Host Disease:** This esophagitis is caused by a surgical procedure, mostly after a bone marrow transplant. The body gets attacked by the newly transplanted cells and causes esophagitis.

Diagnosing Esophagitis

The medical practitioner in charge of this inflammation type is called a gastroenterologist. There are specific tests ordered by the gastroenterologist to check the ailment; some of these tests are;

Esophageal Manometry: The purpose of this test is to measure the pressure in the esophagus' lower part. A pressure-sensitive tube (a very thin tube) is taken into the stomach through the mouth. After it gets into the stomach, the tube gets pulled back into the esophagus slowly. During this test, it is required of patients to swallow. While they swallow, the pressure of muscle contractions is measured.

· · ·

Esophagogastroduodenoscopy (EGD): During this test, the gastroenterologist utilizes an endoscope to check the esophagus directly. The examination is also done on the first part of the intestines and the stomach. Additionally, samples of tissue are attained to get the extent of damage the esophagus has taken.

Barium Swallow Or Upper GI Series: During this test, x-rays of the esophagus is taken after the patient has swallowed a barium solution. The lining of the esophagus is coated by barium. It is displayed on an x-ray as white. The barium solution reveals where the esophagus is affected. It also shows the amount of damage taken by the esophagus.

Causes Of Esophagitis

Esophagitis is caused by esophagus irritation, infection, and of course, inflammation of the esophagus lining. However, one of the major causes of this ailment is stomach acid reflux. Reflux is caused by several things like;

Vomiting: Frequent vomiting causes acid damage to the esophagus. Persistent vomiting causes little tears in the inner lining of the esophagus; this causes more damage to the esophagus. That week feeling you get during and after vomiting is probably the small "tears" in your esophagus taking their toll on you, except, of course, the fact that food is exiting your body through the wrong means.

Hiatal Hernia: Hiatal hernia is an abnormal occurrence caused when a part of the stomach goes atop the diaphragm.

This move causes the production of a little abdominal pouch. This pouch is called a hiatal hernia.

ACHALASIA: This is experienced when there is an abnormal opening of the esophagus' lower end. When this happens, food's movement gets restricted in the esophagus, or the food regurgitates. This can cause a temporary restriction of airflow. This condition increases the risk of esophageal cancer.

IRONICALLY, treating other ailments can cause esophageal irritation. Certain surgical procedures like weight loss surgery can heighten the risk of esophagitis in a person. Anti-inflammatory drugs like aspirin can cause irritation in the esophagus lining.

ESOPHAGITIS CAUSED by drug intake occurs when individuals use little water to take large pills before bed. These drugs get stuck in the esophagus after getting dissolved. Cancer treatment like chest radiation can cause develop burns that eventually become scars and irritate the esophagus.

More Causes Of Esophagitis

There are more causes of esophagitis. Yes, the causes of esophagitis are so much because the esophagus is a very sensitive part of the human body that gets utilized daily. Every human must swallow something daily, so you must be familiar with as many causes as possible. Some of these causes include; smoking, swallowing toxic substances or things that should not go in the human body, and swallowing foods with excessive caffeine and acid.

Treatment Of Esophagitis

Treating esophagitis is totally dependent on what caused it; the ailment can be treated with endoscopy, lifestyle and diet changes, surgery, dilation of the esophagus.

THE SYMPTOMS of this ailment can be significantly lessened by diet. The GERD diet ensures the reduction of the main cause of this ailment, which is acid reflux.

MANY OVER-THE-COUNTER DRUGS can enable the neutralization of stomach acid; they also offer relief for the pain, albeit for a short while. However, it is recommended that you do not take these drugs for too long if esophagitis persists. You should visit a doctor instead.

Medical Treatment

Regardless of the treatments mentioned earlier, it is best to get proper treatment from the hospital. The cause of esophagitis depends on the cause, and as we know by this point, there are many causes.

- Infection-induced esophagitis is medically treated with a focus on getting the infection cured.
- Acid reflux induced esophagitis is medically treated to block or slow down acid production
- Esophagitis caused by surgeries is treated with the elongated intake of acid-blocking medications.
- Esophagitis caused by medications is treated with better medications (medications that are compatible with the affected patient).

- Endoscopy can be used to remove any lodged pill fragments, food, or foreign bodies stuck in the esophagus. Stretching (dilatation) of the esophagus can also be done as part of the endoscopy procedure.
- Surgery may be necessary to remove any damaged portions of the esophagus. In the case of Barrett's esophagus, where the risk of cancer is increased, surgery might be the treatment of choice.
- Eosinophilic esophagitis is treated with gentle stretching of the esophagus (dilatation) and medications to decrease white blood cells (eosinophils) in the esophagus lining.
- Achalasia may be treated with stretching of the esophagus (dilatation) when oral medications fail to improve symptoms.

Foods That Help With Esophagitis

There are types of foods that can agitate or delineate esophagitis. Here are some of them below.

Foods That Delineate Esophagitis

Foods that help to soothe esophagitis include protein meals, soft and easily digested food, and foods of small quantity (to be eaten frequently).

Foods And Drinks That Agitates Esophagitis

Foods that enhance the symptoms of esophagitis are spicy foods that worsen or cause heartburn (garlic, mint, chocolate, and onions), caffeinated foods, and acidic foods (tomatoes and citrus).

Lifestyle Changes That Can Help With Esophagitis

Earlier I mentioned that lifestyle changes will help with esophagitis; some of these life style changes include;

- Shed some weight
- If you smoke, then you should stop
- Eat with small bites and munch your meals gingerly
- Sit upright during and after eating
- Do not eat three hours before bed
- Stay away from NSAIDs (nonsteroidal anti-inflammatory drugs) like naproxen, ibuprofen, and aspirin.

Esophagitis Complications

GERD-induced esophagitis can cause chronic scarring, ulcers, and bleeding if it is not treated on time. Such chronic scarring can lead to narrowing the esophagus, which will deter the patient's ability to swallow even the most tender foods.

ONE OF THE most predominant complications from esophagitis is Barrett's esophagus. This ailment heightens the risk of esophageal cancer. A serious case of esophagitis may cause malnutrition also.

Treatment Duration

The amount of time it takes for one to recover from esophagitis depends on what caused the condition; as we have learned so far from this book, esophagitis is caused by different things. Some of these causes are more chronic than others, and that affects the recovery period.

. . .

INFLAMMATION-INDUCED esophagitis (which this book is focused on) can be treated with behavioral changes, surgery, and medications. The recovery period for most people is short, while others take a longer time to recover.

Preventing Esophagitis

Just like most inflammation types, esophagitis can be prevented. You can change your lifestyle and diet to avoid getting esophagitis. Oral hygiene is very important in esophagitis; maintaining proper hygiene can help to prevent esophagitis. Finally, when taking pills, ensure they are taken with a lot of water.

COPD and Inflammation

COPD is an acronym for Chronic Obstructive Pulmonary Disease (COPD). It is an inflammatory disease that causes difficulty in breathing. It affects the lung and lingers on for a long time.

Types of COPD

COPD is a term mostly utilized in the description of a plethora of conditions that affect the lungs; some of these conditions include;

CHRONIC BRONCHITIS: The bronchial cubes of every person have hair-like fibers that aid in the movement of mucus; these fibers are called the cilia line. Chronic Bronchitis occurs when the cilia are no longer there. An affected individual has diffi-

culty breathing, coughs incessantly, and their mucus becomes excessive and lingers longer than necessary.

EMPHYSEMA: This ailment occurs when an individual's alveoli are damaged. This causes the obliteration of the alveoli (air sacs) wall and morphs into one colossal air sac. When this merger occurs, the alveoli have difficulties absorbing oxygen, and the oxygen that goes to your blood becomes minimal. The lungs will lose their springiness and stretch out when the alveoli are damaged, causing difficulties in breathing.

REFRACTORY ASTHMA: This is basically asthma, but it is the worse kind as normal asthma medications have no effect.

Cause Of COPD

The major cause of this type of inflammation is smoking. The lungs get irritated by anything that is smoke-related and begins to tighten up. Even if you do not smoke, hanging around individuals that smoke and inhaling their "puffs" can also cause COPD. If you are asthmatic and also smoke, then you are at higher risk of getting affected.

ALTHOUGH THE MOST common cause of COPD is smoking, exposure to certain chemicals (for too long), air pollution, and dust can also cause inflammation. Age plays a great role in this ailment as it does not manifest immediately. The components of the disease accumulate over time, and the symptoms become obvious around forty years.

Symptoms Of COPD

As mentioned earlier, COPD is a pretty sneaky disease as the symptoms do not show immediately, but as the condition worsens, the symptoms begin to manifest. These are some of the symptoms that occur when COPD begins to worsen;

- Persistent coughing
- Breathing difficulties despite being fit
- Blue fingernails
- Congested feeling in the chest
- Cough induced mucus
- Squeaking or wheezing while breathing
- Weakness
- Incessant flu or cold
- Swelling in the legs, feet, and ankles
- Losing weight unintentionally (this occurs when the condition becomes severe)

Diagnosing COPD

When a doctor notices any signs of COPD in a patient, the doctor asks the patient if they have been exposed to dust, chemicals, or smoke at the office. The doctor also asks for medical history and asks if the patient smokes. A physical exam and breathing tests will be carried. As a patient, it is important to let the doctor know if you have a persistent cough. Even if the cough is not persistent yet, just speak up if you have a cough.

SPIROMETRY IS the most popular test method for this ailment. The patient is required to breathe into a large flexible tube. The tube is directly linked to a machine known as a spirometer. The

spirometer ascertains the strength of the lungs by measuring how much air it can hold.

COPD Treatments

Unfortunately, there is no known cure for COPD. The only way to manage it is to slow it down and ease the symptoms. Any complications COPD causes in a patient get treated to ensure you have a better life.

IT IS A NO-BRAINER, but the most important step towards managing COPD is to stop smoking. Although it is a difficult habit to let go, with the help of a doctor and the patient's will, it is achievable.

BELOW ARE TREATMENTS FOR COPD:

CORTICOSTEROIDS: These drugs are utilized in the reduction of inflammation in the airways. They can either be swallowed as pills or inhaled.

ROFLUMILAST: An enzyme called PDE4 is embedded in this drug. PDE4 keeps people with COPD from flaring up.

BRONCHODILATORS: These drugs are inhaled to get the airways opened up. Inhaling them is the best way to take them.

.   .   .

ANTIBIOTICS: These are prescribed by doctors to battle bacterial infections.

COMBINATION INHALERS: This inhaler is a pairing of a bronchodilator and steroids

OXYGEN THERAPY: This is imperative. It helps to eradicate breathing difficulties, safeguards the organs, and ensures a better life. This treatment is mostly applied to chronic cases.

PULMONARY REHABILITATION: This is a rehabilitation program that includes disease management, counseling, and exercise that ensures the patient is as active and healthy as they can be.

PNEUMONIA OR FLU VACCINES: These vaccines are administered to patients to reduce the risk of COPD.

SURGERY: When COPD is severe in a patient, surgery will be suggested by the doctor, and different procedures can be done.

Surgical Procedures

Lung Volume Reduction Surgery: This procedure is done to remove the affected lung tissue

BULLECTOMY: This procedure is done to remove bullae and the colossal air spaces that break down the alveoli.

. . .

LUNG TRANSPLANT: This is done in the most severe cases. The affected lung is removed, and a new one is inserted into the patient.

COPD Complications

COPD is beyond a dangerous ailment; it can cause other health issues in patients if not properly managed. Here are some health issues COPD can cause:

LUNG CANCER: COPD increases the chance of getting lung cancer

RESPIRATORY INFECTIONS: When the lung is broken down by COPD, the patient is susceptible to pneumonia, the flu, and colds. These ailments increase your breathing difficulties and agitate your already existing case of COPD.

HIGH BLOOD PRESSURE: The blood pressure of a patient with COPD may spike. This condition is called pulmonary hypertension.

HEART PROBLEMS: Although the reason is yet to be detected by doctors, the risk of heart disease is heightened when a patient has COPD. It can even lead to a heart attack in the long run.

DEPRESSION: This is a no-brainer. A serious ailment like COPD can leave a person depressed. The patient will not function like

they used to due to shortness of breath will eventually take its toll on them.

Life With COPD

The fact that COPD has no cure has already been established; however, there are lifestyle choices a patient can make that will ensure a great lifestyle. If these choices are followed judiciously, the patient expends his or her complete life span. Here are things that can help patients live with COPD.

- Stop smoking! This has been mentioned a plethora of times because it is the main cause of this ailment.
- Ensure medications are taken according to directions
- Engage in breathing exercises
- Stay away from air pollution, dust, and fumes
- Go for medical check-ups regularly
- Join a support group or go for counseling for emotional support
- Engage in light exercises weekly. It does not have to be daily but ensure it is done weekly
- Ensure your diet is healthy
- Clear your lungs with plenty of water, controlled coughing, and a humidifier.

COPD Flares

This falls under "life with COPD," sometimes symptoms of COPD flare up for weeks or days. When this happens, the patient may cough with more mucus, or the breathing difficulties get to an all-time high. This is referred to as acute exacerbation by doctors. If it is not treated on time, it may degenerate to lung failure.

. . .

THIS CAN BE TREATED with steroids or antibiotics. Oxygen treatment is also effective. However, the patient may need to go to the hospital. When you recover from this, you must follow these steps to avoid the flares from occurring again.

- Stay away from air pollution
- Stop smoking!
- Ensure you take pneumonia and flu vaccines annually
- Long-acting bronchodilators, inhaled steroids, and other medications prescribed by the doctor should be taken

COPD is a very serious ailment and should be taken seriously in its early stages. It is one of the strongest aftermaths of inflammation. Endeavor to live a healthy lifestyle devoid of smoking (yes, I said it again) to prevent this from happening.

Arthritis and Inflammation

Arthritis occurs when a person's joint is inflamed. When this occurs, the individual experiences soreness, soreness, stiffness, and especially swelling in the affected area. Although there are many types of arthritis, the most popular forms of arthritis are noninflammatory and inflammatory arthritis. Rheumatoid Arthritis (RA) is one of the most popular arthritis types.

Cause Of Arthritis

For the purpose of this book, I will focus on inflammatory arthritis, which is rheumatoid arthritis. This type of arthritis

affects the hands mostly. Patients feel pains in their wrists, hands, knees, feet, elbows, and ankles.

RHEUMATOID ARTHRITIS IS AN AUTOIMMUNE DISEASE, and what causes this ailment has remained a mystery since its discovery. However, experts believe that the cause of this disease stems from genetic, hormonal factors as the ailment affects women more than men. Rare cases of rheumatoid arthritis appear in kids; apart from joints, rheumatoid arthritis can attack other parts of the body like the lungs and eyes. It is indeed a fascinating condition.

Symptoms Of Arthritis

Signs of rheumatoid arthritis occur when the affected individual has swelling, pain, and stiffness in the joints. The stiffness lasts for a really long time, and it hurts mostly when the affected individual just wakes up in the morning.

THE SYMPTOMS of rheumatoid arthritis transcend beyond pains in the joint. It includes fatigue and weakness.

Arthritis Diagnosis

The first thing the doctor usually does on a patient suspected to have arthritis is to examine the joints, then screening tests are ordered.

SOFT TISSUES in the joints of a patient are unveiled by an MRI. Erosions, cartilage breakdown, and bone damage are exposed by standard X-rays.

. . .

AFTER DETECTING THE JOINT PROBLEM, the doctor ordered a blood test to ascertain if rheumatoid arthritis is the cause of the joint issues.

Treatment For Rheumatoid Arthritis

Although doctors may recommend corticosteroids and NSAIDs to patients with RA Rheumatoid Arthritis), but there designated drugs for the ailment. Some of the drugs are discussed below.

JANUS KINASE INHIBITORS: This drug shuts down specific immune system responses to prohibit joint damage and inflammation.

DISEASE-MODIFYING ANTIRHEUMATIC DRUGS: These are referred to as DMARDs; they slow down the progression of this ailment by prohibiting the body's immune system.

BIOLOGICS: instead of prohibiting the immune system and deterring it from working, these drugs tackle the part of the immune system that leads to inflammation.

AS EXPERTS CONTINUE to study this condition, there have been tests of new drugs that can reduce the pains that come with rheumatoid arthritis. Drugs that will treat it are also currently under development. Physical therapy also plays a great role in relieving the pains that come with rheumatoid arthritis.

Life With Arthritis

Living with arthritis is no walk in the park, but it is possible. Losing weight and engaging in regular exercise can take away the pains on the joints of an affected person. Exercise is the most important of the two. It aids weight loss and helps to strengthen the muscles around the affected joints.

DEVICES LIKE RAISED TOILET SEATS, canes, and other equipment can be used by patients with severe cases. This equipment helps the affected person go through their daily activities.

AS WE HAVE COME to understand, a good diet helps with inflammation, and the case is not different with arthritis. Healthy diets that include low-fat proteins, vegetables, fruits, and grains help the affected patient keep a healthy weight and ease inflammation.

ALTHOUGH NO CURE has been detected yet for this inflammation, it can be managed. Getting it treated on time will ensure the best results. A plethora of individuals credits joint pains and stiffness in their bodies to their body aging. If you notice these pains incessantly, you must visit the doctor's office as they may be arthritis symptoms.

INTENTIONAL TREATMENT and understanding what a patient is going through will ensure proper management of arthritis. The patient will be comfortable and active for years.

Lymphedema and Inflammation

Lymphedema is a condition that occurs when the lymphatic system in the human body starts to malfunction. This malfunction leads to an inflammatory process that manifests as secondary malignancy, recurrent infections, and uneasiness.

THE LYMPHATIC SYSTEM in a person consists of lymph vessels, and lymph nodes, the fluids from the body's tissues are drained by the lymph nodes and vessels. Toxins, waste products, and immune cells are inside the fluids and are transported to the lymph nodes. Fluid balance is maintained in the body by lymph vessels; this is achieved via the return of filtered lymph to a person's bloodstream.

WHEN THE LYMPHATIC system is not working properly, the fluid fills up the tissues, which causes them to swell. When this happens, the affected person's arms and legs get swollen, affecting other body parts. In some cases, individuals can be born with a problem that causes the ailment. This type of lymphedema is called primary or hereditary lymphedema. A plethora of genetic conditions cause this type of lymphedema.

HOWEVER, since our focus is on lymphedema and inflammation, primary lymphedema will be ignored. Lymphedema can be developed from an injury or complications from the disease. This type of inflammation usually happens after complications from surgery to treat cancer caused by inflammation. So here we see the connection between lymphedema and inflammation. This type of lymphedema is called secondary lymphedema.

Causes Of Lymphedema

As aforementioned, lymphedema is caused by complications from injury or surgical procedures. One of the most popular causes of this ailment is breast cancer treatment with a mastectomy. During this procedure, lymph tissue is extracted beneath the patient's hand during the removal of cancerous breast tissue. If lymph modes are extracted in the process, it causes lymphedema in the arm.

TREATMENT OF AILMENTS like cancer of the neck (caused by chronic esophagitis) can cause lymphedema. This is a chromic case as it leads to swelling on the lips, face, neck, and eyes.

Symptoms Of Lymphedema

The symptoms of this disease are quite obvious as the affected areas get swollen. However, there are other symptoms apart from swelling that must be watched out for.

- Blisters
- Discoloration of skin
- Infection
- Leakage of fluids from the skin

When one has lymphedema in the neck and head, the individual's vision might be impaired. The individual will experience pain in the ears and nasal congestion. Other issues caused by lymphedema in the head and neck include;

- Difficulty to speak
- Breathing difficulties
- Struggling to swallow food

Individuals with secondary lymphedema may experience it any time after the surgical procedure that prompted it. However, it may not happen immediately; some occur months after while others occur some years later.

Lymphedema Diagnosis

During tests for lymphedema, a physical exam is performed by a doctor. The doctor also asks for the individual's medical history. If the doctor suspects lymphedema, imaging tests are ordered.

Treatment For Lymphedema

The aim of treating this ailment is to significantly reduce swelling in the early stages or as soon as the affected person has been diagnosed with the ailment. The treatments for lymphedema include;

- **Compression**

This is a very vital treatment method for this ailment. The affected limbs are compressed; this is done so that the lymphatic fluids can return to their normal circulation pattern.

Compression is mostly effective when the limbs of the patient are affected as opposed to other areas. The limbs are sturdily wrapped with a bandage made of elastic. This can also be achieved by using a compression garment. The compression garment is worn by the patient and constantly exerts pressure on the affected area.

- **Lymphatic Drainage Massage**

This treatment is a massage therapy procedure where a

Anti-Inflammatory Diet for Beginners 29

qualified lymphedema professional manipulates the tissues to ensure free drainage of the lymph fluids. This is effective for all body parts. It is mostly beneficial for lymphedema that affects the face, neck, and lips because the compression will not work in that case.

The severity of the condition and swelling location determines how often a lymphatic drainage massage is required. Self-sufficient patients can also get professional training to do this massage at home, but I do not recommend that. Manual drainage must be avoided if you have skin infections like cellulitis.

- **Liposuction**

When all else fails, surgery is the best solution; liposuction is a great option to eliminate the fluids. It is mostly needed when the ailment is advanced.

Life With Lymphedema

The probable future with lymphedema depends on the location (affected area), cause, the severity, and the patient's overall health. Like most of the inflammation-induced ailments in this book so far, lymphedema is a condition that needs constant care. Some individuals encounter sporadic swelling even after treatment, but it can be put under control.

WORKING with a lymphedema expert team is imperative; this team must consist of medical experts, surgical experts, and physical therapists. Using a conglomeration of management techniques and treatments is the best way to tackle this condition.

Inflammatory Bowel Disease and Inflammation

Inflammatory Bowel Disease, known mostly as IBD, is a unit of disorders in the intestine. This ailment causes an elongated inflammation of the digestive tract. For the benefit of those who have no idea what the digestive tract is, it comprises the stomach, mouth, small intestine, esophagus, and large intestine.

THE DIGESTIVE TRACT makes it possible to digest meals by having food nutrients extracted and getting rid of waste products and useless material. The normal digestive process is intercepted when inflammation happens anywhere in the tract. IBD is a disruptive and painful ailment. It can be fatal in extreme cases.

Types Of IBD

According to the Crohn's & Colitis Foundation Of America (CCFA), an estimated 1.6 million individuals suffer from IBD in the United States. There are a plethora of diseases under IBD. Crohn's disease and Ulcerative Colitis are two of the most common.

ULCERATIVE COLITIS OCCURS when there is inflammation of the large intestine. Crohn's disease, on the other hand, has no limits as inflammation can occur anywhere in the digestive tract.

Causes Of IBD

Medical practitioners are yet to ascertain the main cause of this ailment, but there are risk factors for the development of

Crohn's disease and Ulcerative Colitis (UC), some of these risk factors include;

GENETICS AND FAMILY HISTORY: Your odds of getting IBD are heightened if you have a family member with it.

SMOKING: One of the risk factors for Crohn's disease is smoking. Symptoms and pain caused by Crohn's disease are aggravated by smoking. UC, on the other hand, is mostly experienced by non-smokers.

THE IMMUNE SYSTEM: Like most inflammatory diseases, the immune system has a role to play in Inflammatory Bowel Disease. An immune response can be triggered by a viral or bacterial infection of the tract. When this response occurs, there is inflammation in the digestive tract. When the immune response is normal, the inflammation subsides after the infection has been tackled.

HOWEVER, digestive tract inflammation can occur with or without infection in individuals with Inflammatory Bowel Disease.

ETHNICITY: Although this ailment affects everyone, people of certain ethnic groups have heightened chances of getting it. According to a report, Ashkenazi Jews, white people, and people of other specific ethnicities are likely to have IBD. There has been a heightened increase in IBD rates among Black individuals in Britain.

. . .

GENDER: Although IBD affects both genders at the same rate, there are a few exceptions. Men over the age of forty-five are likely to have UC instead of their female counterparts of the same age. Women and girls over fourteen years old mostly get affected by Crohn's disease.

AGE: IBD does not affect people at any specific age, but it begins before an individual gets to thirty-five years in most cases.

THE ENVIRONMENT: According to research, individuals who dwell in industrialized countries and urban areas are more likely to have IBD. Individuals who dwell in northern climates have a high chance of IBD. According to research, a sedentary job or lifestyle may increase your chance of IBD.

HOWEVER, studies have proven that having a healthy exercise lifestyle delineates the chances of an individual from having IBD.

Symptoms Of IBD

The severity and location of inflammation determine the symptoms of IBD. Here are the symptoms:

BLEEDING ULCERS: Individuals will excrete feces with blood on them.

. . .

Anti-Inflammatory Diet for Beginners 33

DIARRHEA: This is when water cannot be reabsorbed by the bowel parts that have been affected.

EMACIATION: individuals will lose weight at an alarming rate. This may lead to slow physical growth in children.

INDIVIDUALS WHO SUFFER from Crohn's disease experience canker sores in their oral opening. Other times fissures and ulcers also show in the anus or genitalia area.

ALTHOUGH IBD IS a digestive tract dysfunction, symptoms can be seen in areas not connected to the digestive system. These areas are arthritis, inflammation in the eye, and skin disorders.

Diagnosis Of IBD

When an individual goes to the doctor's office to test for IBD, the doctor asks for bowel movements and family history. The doctor carries out a physical exam and more tests. Here are some of the tests below.

BARIUM ENEMA: This test has become somewhat obsolete in recent times; it is an exam of the small intestine and colon.

BLOOD TEST AND STOOL SAMPLE: Doctors order blood tests to ascertain if an individual is suffering from Crohn's disease and UC. Stool samples are used to ascertain if an individual has other underlying diseases and infections apart from IBD.

. . .

CAPSULE ENDOSCOPY: For this test, the individual swallows a capsule that has a camera in it. This test is meant to inspect the small intestine. After swallowing the capsule, the camera takes photos as it passes the small intestine. The pictures are seen after the individual has passed excreta. This test is usually a last resort. It is employed when other tests have flopped in finding the cause of Crohn's disease.

COLONOSCOPY AND FLEXIBLE SIGMOIDOSCOPY: During this procedure, a then flexible probe with a camera embedded is used to look at the colon. The anus is the insertion point of the camera. The doctor searches for fistulas, ulcers, and other abnormalities in the rectum.

X-RAY OR PLAIN FILM: Doctors use a plain abdominal x-ray in the case of an emergency. This emergency is mostly when the doctors suspect an intestinal rupture.

MRI AND CT SCANS: MRIs are safer as opposed to X-rays since radiation is not needed. They detect fistulas by examining soft tissues. CT scans are an X-ray with a computer. The images gotten from a CT scan are clearer than those gotten from a normal X-ray.

MRIs AND CT scans both help the doctor ascertain the areas of the intestine IBD has affected.

Treatment For Inflammatory Bowel Disease

A plethora of treatments has been developed to treat IBD.

- **Lifestyle Choices**

When a person has been diagnosed with IBD, lifestyle choices play an important role. Drinking a lot of liquid makes up for the fluids absent in your stool. Quit smoking and develop an exercise habit, and one must stay away from dairy products as much as possible.

- **Medications**

THE FIRST STEP of treating IBD is anti-inflammatory drugs. Inflammation of the digestive tract is reduced by these medications.

CORTICOSTEROIDS: Although corticosteroids are not directly used, glucocorticoids, a sub-category of the drug, are used. Some other drugs that are sub-categories of corticosteroids are prednisone, budesonide, methylprednisolone, and prednisolone.

THE DRUGS MENTIONED ABOVE ARE available in several forms like vaccines, oral tablets, and rectal foams. They are administered for a short time, and the doses are usually small.

5-ASA DRUGS: Inflammation is reduced by 5-ASA drugs. 5-ASA drugs include olsalazine, balsalazide, sulfasalazine, and

mesalamine. The American Gastroenterological Association dropped some treatment instructions for adults who have UC in 2019. The instructions were:

DIAZO-BONDED 5-ASA *drugs like olsalazine and balsalazide* and *standard-dose oral mesalamine*

THE DRUGS MENTIONED ABOVE ARE BETTER than low-dose sulfasalazine, mesalamine, or no treatment. According to the Association, sulfasalazine can be taken as long as the patient is aware of the side effects.

IMMUNOMODULATORS: This drug is used when 5-ASA drugs and corticosteroids are insufficient to get the job done. The function of immunomodulators is to stop the immune system from causing inflammation to the bowels. Immunomodulators include azathioprine, methotrexate, and mercaptopurine.

ALTHOUGH IMMUNOMODULATORS ARE YET to be approved by the Food And Drug Administration (FDA), they can be prescribed by the doctor.

BIOLOGICS: These are drugs genetically designed for individuals with acute to chronic cases of IBD. Tumor Necrosis Factor (TNF) is blocked by some of these biologics. TNF is an inflammation-causing chemical that the immune system produces. Naturally, there is blockage of excess in the blood, but that is not the case with people with IBD. Inflammation can happen when there is a high TNF level. Apart from TNF, there are

other biologics like natalizumab (Tysabri), certolizumab (cimzia), vedolizubab (entyzio), and ustekinubab (stelara).

TREATMENT GUIDELINES WERE RELEASED by the AGA in 2020 for individuals with moderate to severe UC. The AGA recommended vedolizumab or infliximab instead of adalimumab for individuals who have never used a biologic.

OTHER DRUGS: Pathways that cause inflammation are blocked by other drugs. The AGA has recommended that tofacitinib (xeijanz) be used only in a registry or clinical study. This was recommended with safety in mind. Antibiotics are also effective as they eradicate bacteria in the small intestine that has the probability of worsening Crohn's symptoms. Laxatives and antidiarrheal medications are also effective in eradicating the symptoms of IBD.

SUPPLEMENTS: Mineral supplements and vitamins are effective against nutritional deficiencies. Anemia can be treated with iron supplements. However, you must consult a doctor before using any new supplement.

SURGERY: In heightened cases, surgery is the only option left to treat IBD. Here are the surgeries used to treat IBD: removal or closure of fistulas, narrowed bowel widening via strictureplasty, and ejecting the rectum and colon.

3

CHAPTER THREE: HOW INFLAMMATION IS MEASURED

There are a lot of theories out there about the things that can generally reduce or influence inflammation. The causes of different types of inflammation have been explored in this book. Still, there are several ways to measure and reduce inflammation before it escalates.

To HELP you understand how inflammation is measured, I will highlight certain things (some have already been addressed) you must understand about inflammation.

SPECIFIC THINGS You Must Understand About Inflammation

- Your diet and eating habits have a great effect on inflammation. However, one must stick with strategies that are backed up by research instead of relying on contextually misguided lab studies.
- Cancer, high blood pressure, and heart disease can all be caused by chronic low-grade inflammation.

- Chronic inflammation is measured by tests like hsCRP.

SCIENTISTS STUDY how the overall well-being of an individual is affected by inflammation. Then, they come up with ways to eradicate it. A CRP test is one of the ways inflammation is measured by experts.

CRP Test

A CRP test is one of the most effective ways inflammation is measured; CRP (C-reactive protein) is produced in the liver. Doctors carry out a CRP test to identify heightened inflammation levels like the ones present in lupus and rheumatoid arthritis. However, low-grade inflammation cannot be detected by a Regular CRP. Doctors use high-sensitivity CRP (hs-CRP) for the detection of low-grade inflammation.

WHEN DECISIONS CAN BE GUIDED By A CRP Test

- Individuals that have **intermediate or borderline risk** can have their decisions influenced by hsCRP. This will determine their preventive interventions.
- Individuals with **coronary artery disease** have to be extra careful because excessive hsCRPs may increase the chance of cardiovascular event within the next half-decade; this means that the person has a high chance of cardiac arrests. According to researchers, lipid-lowering and inflammation-inhibiting lifestyle should be combined to ensure inflammation does not

escalate and eventually dissipate before it becomes fully blown.

CHRONIC INFLAMMATION: **The Warning Sign**

In this text, it has been established that chronic inflammation is a severe type of inflammation instead of acute inflammation. Chronic inflammation is a proverbial warning sign because;

- It plays a role in the destabilization and development of blood vessels atherosclerotic plaque.
- Vascular remodeling is promoted by inflammation in the blood vessels. This can cause the arteries to be stiff.
- It can lead to cancer in severe cases, and cancer can be fatal.
- Human DNA can be damaged by inflammation; this is where cancer develops.
- Cancer progression can be promoted via many metabolic pathways.

4

CHAPTER FOUR: REDUCTION OF INFLAMMATION

In recent years, more concern has been channeled to inflammation, and this is with good reason. As highlighted in this text, inflammation causes a lot of damage to the body. Apart from adopting an inflammatory diet, there are a plethora of ways inflammation can be reduced. Inflammation reduction activities can reduce joint pain, autoimmune diseases, dementia, diabetes, heart disease, cancer, Alzheimer's disease, and the aging process.

THE BEST THING about inflammation reduction methods is that the results are seen daily, and there is no need to wait for months. Follow these eleven guidelines to reduce inflammation.

1. **Eat Salad Daily:** Develop a habit of carrying a package of leafy greens wherever you go. You do not have to eat the salad alone; it can be added to your meals once on twice a day. All you need to do is

ensure that the salad gets into your body. Leafy greens like arugula, lettuce, or baby spinach are great choices for daily consumption. The aforementioned leafy greens have bioactive compounds and antioxidants that offer anti-inflammatory double-punch.

2. **Balanced Snacking:** This may be difficult for more people than others but avoid sweetened coffee drinks and the vending machine as much as possible. If you crave a quick snack, go for a snack that is rich in fiber. You can have veggies, hummus, cheese cubes, and snacks with a small amount of protein like peanut butter and apple slices. A balanced snacking habit is one of the keys to keep blood sugar within normal parameters; this helps you avoid irritability, cravings, and hunger. Apart from being good for people around you (they will have a healthy friend or family member), it eradicates inflammation that can cause type 2 diabetes, obesity, and heart disease.

3. **Sleep On Time:** Today, there are so many distractions like Netflix and social media, and they contribute to late nights in individuals. Ensure you leave social media and get off Netflix to go to bed on time; the required 7 to 8 hours of sleep for an adult is very imperative for your overall well-being. Inflammation can be triggered when an individual does not get enough sleep, and it can still occur if the person is in good health. Inflammation developed from sleeplessness can cause Alzheimer's, type 2 diabetes, obesity, dementia, and heart disease.

4. **Take A Walk:** This can be overlooked if you have a

Anti-Inflammatory Diet for Beginners 43

daily workout routine, but you can do it on days you miss your workout. According to research in 2017, inflammatory blood markers can be reduced by twenty minutes of movement. If you have a dog, you can take it for a walk to make the exercise more interesting.

5. **Spice Things Up:** Once in a while, try to add a little garlic or spice when cooking your meals or opt for meals with things like that if you cannot cook. Aromatic and fragrant spices have the potential to eradicate inflammation and the risk of it. According to a study, spices or herbs like rosemary, cumin, fenugreek, turmeric, ginger, and cinnamon decreases inflammation that can cause respiratory issues, degenerative brain conditions, cancer, and heart disease.

6. **Reduce Your Alcohol Intake:** If you have a habit of drinking every day, you should stop that for a few days. This is not a lifetime habit, so there is no need to fret, abstinence from alcohol for a while calms the body down, and existing inflammation is reduced. Although there are some benefits associated with moderate alcohol consumption, many individuals cross the line and expose themselves to inflammation. This point is only effective when combined with other anti-inflammatory lifestyle and diet changes.

7. **Green Tea:** Many individuals drink two to three cups of coffee daily; this can be balanced by swapping one of the coffee cups for a cup of green tea. Green tea is quite healthy as the leaves contain polyphenol compounds that can help reduce inflammation. Apart from inflammation, the risk of

joint conditions, Alzheimer's disease, and cancer can be reduced by taking green tea regularly.

8. **Go Easy On Your Gut**: There are good bacteria already existing in every individual, so probiotics will enhance them. Cut out trans fats and added sugar to safeguard the existing good bacteria. You should put all your attention on minimally processed foods. Probiotic-rich foods like kimchi, kombucha, sauerkraut, miso, or yogurt are also good for you. One of the cornerstones to inflammation reduction is getting the microbe barrier of the gut strengthened.

9. **Fast**: Okay, this is no religious approach or anything. Still, according to research, there are many benefits associated with intermittent fasting (IF). This is because this eating pattern (fasting) induces anti-inflammatory effects. Fasting can be done in many ways, but a 12-hour fast is the easiest way to begin. In the 12-hour fast, finish your dinner at 7 pm and stick to only black coffee or water until 7 am the following day. According to studies, doing intermittent fasting regularly can improve brain health and insulin sensitivity and reduce inflammatory bowel disease and heart disease risk.

10. **Temporarily Cut Out Dairy And Gluten**: Usually, gluten and dairy are barely inflammatory in healthy people, but when inflammation already exists, it can be irritating. Cutting out gluten, dairy, or both for less than a month may benefit several individuals. This is most effective when a diet rich in anti-inflammatory foods is consumed.

11. **Relax**: You may have the healthiest diet in the world, but you cannot get rid of low-grade inflammation if you are constantly on the move. High-stress levels

can increase the risk of inflammation. Even if the stress does not occur daily, mismanaging it when it comes is also an issue. Look for healthy ways to deal with or stay away from stress, like taking a short walk, practicing yoga, or meditating; this gives physiological and psychological relief.

5

CHAPTER FIVE: FOODS AND INFLAMMATION

This book has hinted at the important role food plays in inflammation; in this chapter, the importance of food in dealing with inflammation is elaborated.

Cancer And Inflammatory Diet

Cancer is one of the most severe complications of inflammation; several research has confirmed the role of inflammation in cancer. Colon cancer is one of the types of ailments enhanced by inflammation. However anti-inflammatory diet is very effective against it. Before I elaborate on a healthy gut microbiome, chronic inflammation, and anti-inflammatory foods that can help in the battle against cancer, let us take a look at the basics. For this study of the effect of an anti-inflammatory diet on cancer, I will use *colon cancer (bowel cancer)* as a case study.

BOWEL CANCER IS amongst the top five most common cancer experienced by individuals living in the United Kingdom. It is

ranked as the second-highest cancer killer in the world. The good news about bowel cancer is that it can be treated and cured with early diagnosis.

THE BOWEL IS an important part of the digestive system comprised of the large bowel (rectum and bowel) and the small bowel (small intestine). There is a high tendency that cancer will be experienced in the large bowel; there are rare cases of small bowel cancer.

Causes Of Bowel Cancer

Naturally, there is an orderly process that the body cells follow for division, health, growth, and death. However, when cells divide and grow without order and do not die, then cancer occurs.

SEVERAL CASES of colon cancer originate from benign or non-cancerous known as adenomatous polyps that make up the large intestine's inner walls.

Symptoms Of Bowel Cancer

Symptoms of cancer do not occur when the ailment first begins. Symptoms begin to show as cancer grows. These symptoms are; loose and narrow stools, pain during bowel movements, constipation or diarrhea, gas, abdominal pain, or cramps. Inconsistent stooling, blood in the stool or rectal bleeding, unexplained emaciation, constant urges to stool, irritable bowel syndrome (IBS), weakness, and tiredness.

· · ·

AN INDIVIDUAL'S chances of getting bowel cancer are high if he/she has;

- Type 2 diabetes
- Family history of the disease
- History of non-cancerous growths in your bowel
- Inherited syndromes like Lynch syndrome and familial adenomatous polyposis
- Inflammatory bowel diseases like ulcerative colitis or Crohn's disease
- Unhealthy lifestyle (physical inactivity, bad diet, excessive alcohol intake, and smoking).
- Cancer radiation therapy

Preventing Bowel Cancer

According to research, eating too much red meat can increase your chance of getting bowel cancer. According to the World Health Organization (WHO), red meat is an "all mammalian muscle meat." This mammalian muscle meat includes pork, goat, horse, veal, lamb, mutton, horse, and beef.

ACCORDING to a North Italian population study, people who frequently consume red meat with cheese, eggs, and other foods that contain fat have had heightened chances of developing colon or rectal cancer than their age groups who preferred a diet based on plants.

ACCORDING TO A 2015 REPORT, every 50-gram part of processed meat like salami or bacon consumed daily heightens a person's chance of getting colorectal cancer by 18%. This report was

published by the International Agency for Research on Cancer. Following this research, the World Health Organization classified processed meat as *carcinogenic to humans.*

THE RESEARCH EXPOSES the dietary factors that can be linked to bowel cancer via noninflammatory mechanisms. For instance, the risk of bowel cancer is heightened through processed and red meat; this occurs via heightened levels of haem iron content, N-nitroso compounds gotten via meat processing. According to a study the Loma Linda University, vegetarian diet types reduce colorectal cancer risk.

THE BENEFICIAL COMPOUNDS in plants like polyphenols and antioxidants are protective have been tested and evidently decrease inflammation. It delineates the risk of other diseases. It enhances the mood of an individual and ensures the best quality of life.

How Does Anti-Inflammatory Diet Work Against Cancer?

The human immune system becomes active when a foreign organism like chemical, microbe, and plant pollen gets inside the body. Inflammation is triggered when this happens. The overall health is truly protected by intermittent bouts of inflammation when the foreign organisms that get into the body are truly dangerous.

HOWEVER, inflammation may linger sometimes; some may last for days, weeks, and months even when there is no intruder in the body. When this happens, inflammation becomes detri-

mental to your health. As aforementioned in the book, many diseases like Alzheimer's, arthritis, heart disease, diabetes, and depression have all been linked to chronic inflammation.

THE RIGHT ANT-INFLAMMATORY foods will ensure the risk of illness is reduced. Suppose you constantly opt for the wrong foods or inflammatory foods. In that case, you are at risk of inflammatory disease, and as you already know at this point, there are a lot of them.

IF YOU NEED AN EATING plan that will help you with an anti-inflammatory diet, then the *Mediterranean diet* is a great choice. The Mediterranean diet is high in vegetables, fish, nuts, healthy oils, and whole grains. You can visit a nutritionist to give you a concise anti-inflammatory diet plan. The next section will help you with a beginner's menu for inflammatory diet and the thirteen best anti-inflammatory food.

Inflammatory Foods (Foods You Cannot Eat)

It is quite interesting to think about, but the food you eat can affect inflammation in the human body. Below are foods that can cause inflammation.

Food With High-Fructose Corn Syrup And Sugar

The two main types of added sugar in the western diet are high fructose corn syrup and table sugar. Sugar has fifty percent fructose and glucose. High fructose syrup, on the other hand, has fifty-five percent fructose and forty-five percent glucose. Added sugars are dangerous because they can lead to disease by increasing inflammation.

Anti-Inflammatory Diet for Beginners   51

. . .

ACCORDING TO RESEARCH, an animal that consumed a high fructose diet developed breast cancer that traveled to the lungs. This happened because of the body's inflammatory response to sugar.

ANOTHER STUDY SHOWS that high sugar diets debilitate the anti-inflammatory effects of omega-3 fatty acids. Another random trial was made where individuals were made to drink water, regular soda, or diet soda. There were heightened levels of uric acid in those that drank regular soda. Uric acid drives insulin and inflammation resistance. Sugar supplies too much fructose, and that makes it very harmful.

VEGETABLES AND FRUITS have small amounts of fructose are safe to take as it will not aid inflammation. However, added sugars is not a good idea especially when it is in large amounts. Consumption of too much fructose can cause diabetes, chronic kidney disease, cancer, insulin resistance, and fatty liver disease.

ACCORDING TO EXPERTS, inflammation is caused by fructose within the endothelial cells. This can lead to heart disease. Consumption of high fructose can spike inflammatory markers in humans.

FOODS with a high amount of added sugar include; soft drinks, doughnuts, certain cereals, chocolate, sweet pastries, and cookies.

Seed And Vegetable Oils

There was a hundred and thirty percent spike in vegetable oil consumption during in 20th century United States. According to some scientists, vegetable oils like soybean oil influence inflammation because they have omega-6 fatty acid content in abundance. Even though there is a need for some dietary omega-6 fats, the western diet has more than should be consumed.

IT IS RECOMMENDED by health professionals that foods with omega-3, like fatty fish, should be consumed more. This improves the omega-6 to omega-3 ratio and ensures the anti-inflammatory benefits of omega-3s are gained. Although there is limited evidence that excessive consumption of omega-6 fatty acids heightens inflammation in people, the little evidence is enough for individuals to stay away.

ACCORDING TO SOME CONTROLLED STUDIES, inflammatory markers are not affected by linoleic acid. However, more evidence is needed to reach a final and definite conclusion. A lot of processed foods use vegetable and seed oils as cooking oils.

Foods With Artificial Trans Fats

Fats are generally unhealthy, but artificial trans fats are one of the generals. Artificial trans fats are gotten through the addition of hydrogen to unsaturated fats. Trans fats are identified partially as hydrogenated oils on ingredient labels. Trans fats are present in most margarine; they are used in processed foods to ensure longevity.

. . .

NATURAL TRANS FATS are found in meat and dairy. Still, they are not as harmful as artificial trans fat that increases the risk of disease, and cause inflammation. Apart from reducing HDL cholesterol, the function of endothelial cells lining the arteries can be impaired by artificial trans fats (this can cause heart disease in serious cases).

HIGH INFLAMMATORY MARKER levels like C-reactive protein (CRP) are heightened by the consumption of artificial fats. Inflammation is significantly increased by hydrogenated soybean oil compared to sunflower and palm oils.

MEN with elevated cholesterol levels and healthy men have experienced increased inflammatory markers when they consume trans fats.

FOODS THAT CONTAIN excess amounts of trans fats include certain pastries, packaged cookies and cakes, French fries, fried fast food, microwave popcorn, vegetable shortenings, and every processed food with hydrogenated oil listed on the label.

Foods With Refined Carbohydrates

The average human has heard about how bad carbohydrate is for them, but some carbs·are not problematic. Humans used to consume unprocessed carbs with high fiber; most of these unprocessed carbs include roots, grasses, and fruits.

PROCESSED AND REFINED CARBS, on the other hand, may enhance inflammation. Most of the fiber contained in carbs is

removed from refined carbs. The importance of fiber cannot be overlooked. It improves blood sugar control, promotes fullness, and provides feeding for the beneficial bacteria in your gut.

THE PRESENCE of refined carbs in today's diet has the probability of spiking the growth of inflammatory gut bacteria; this heightens your risk of inflammatory bowel disease and obesity. As opposed to unprocessed carbs, there is a higher glycemic index in refined carbs. Blood sugar is rapidly raised more the foods with a low glycemic index.

ACCORDING TO A STUDY, older adults with the highest reported foods with a high glycemic index have a high chance of getting killed by an inflammatory disease like chronic pulmonary disease (COPD).

ANOTHER STUDY REPORTS that healthy young men who consumed 50 grams of refined carbs experienced a spike in certain inflammatory markers and a spike in blood sugar levels.

FOODS with refined carbohydrates include bread, pastries, cookies, sugary soft drinks, cakes, pasta, candy, certain cereals, and processed foods with flour or added sugar.

Alcohol

Moderate consumption of alcohol is beneficial to a person's health and overall well-being, but going overboard is dangerous to health. Too much alcohol intake can lead to an

Anti-Inflammatory Diet for Beginners   55

increase in inflammatory marker CRP levels. The more the alcohol, the more the level of CRP increases.

HEAVY ALCOHOL INTAKE CAN RESULT in problems with bacterial toxins that move into the body from the colon. Alcohol intake should be reduced to two standard drinks daily for men and one drink daily for females; this helps to avoid alcohol-induced health problems.

Processed Meat

The consumption of processed meat can heighten diabetes, heart disease, and colon cancer in individuals. Smoked meat, bacon, sausage, beef jerky, and ham are the most common processed meat.

THERE IS A HIGHER amount of advanced glycation end products (AGEs) in processed meat than other meats, and AGEs cause inflammation. Colon cancer is almost a certainty when you consume processed meat.

THIS BOOK HAS SHOWN that inflammation can be caused by a plethora of triggers. Some of them are really difficult to prevent, like injury, sickness, and pollution. However, the food you eat is totally under your control; that is why it is important to stay away from foods that can cause inflammation.

Anti-Inflammatory Foods (Foods You Can Eat)

This book has talked about inflammation and the scary realities that it can leave behind; if you had never taken this issue

seriously before, I bet you take it very seriously now. Knowing the foods that cause inflammation is just one part of the problem. These foods can be avoided, but what then do you eat? In this section, everything you need to know about anti-inflammatory food will be discussed.

IF YOUR FAVORITE snacks and foods have been struck out as foods that can cause inflammation, don't worry because you will certainly find foods that you can replace those snacks with the foods mentioned here.

Anti-Inflammatory Diet: How It Works

It is only logical that you know how something works before you get involved in it. There is no stipulated diet anywhere by anyone that states what needs to be eaten, how much of it must be eaten, or the time it must be eaten.

HOWEVER, an anti-inflammatory diet mostly consists of meals with foods that have been tested and proven to battle inflammation. Knowledge of such food will help guide how you create a diet for yourself; this is where creativity comes in. There is a diet table in this section to help beginners create an anti-inflammatory diet until they eventually develop a concise one that best suits them.

ACCORDING TO BRITTANY SCANNIELLO, a Colorado-based nutritionist, one should not see an anti-inflammatory diet as just a diet but a lifestyle. Having the mindset that it is a lifestyle as opposed to a diet makes it easier to follow.

· · ·

TO REDUCE the risk of inflammation or aggravate it, it is ideal to consume eight or nine servings of veggies and fruits daily, stay away from simple carbohydrates and opt for complex ones, stay away from dairy and red meat. Of course, processed foods have to be off the menu. Most of these things have been implied in the previous section, but it is imperative to reiterate them.

ENSURE you consume foods that have enough omega-3 fatty acids like halibut, salmon, anchovies, and mussels. Stay with such foods and avoid foods with omega-6 acids embedded in mayonnaise, processed foods, corn oil, salad dressings, and vegetable oil.

AN ANTI-INFLAMMATORY DIET is not relegated to just individuals with inflammation. It is a great diet choice for everybody because foods can cause inflammation (previously discussed). They are bad for the health of a person. So, this diet is great for you. If you care about your overall well-being.

ANYONE DEALING with chronic inflammation must take an anti-inflammatory diet very seriously, as chronic inflammation is the worst kind of inflammation. An anti-inflammatory diet is also beneficial to individuals and athletes who engage in intense exercise and desire to reduce their baseline inflammation.

Research That Has Backed Up The Importance And Effectiveness Of Anti-Inflammatory Diet

There is a plethora of research and evidence that explores and exposes the dangers of inflammation. The most significant

causes of death in the world are diseases caused by chronic inflammation. As mentioned earlier, chronic inflammation causes ailments like obesity, diabetes, and Alzheimer's. Eating foods that cause or enhances inflammation heightens the risk of mortality by over twenty percent; this was published in June 2019 in a meta-analysis.

OTHER RESEARCHERS HAVE STUDIED the effect of indulging in a diet that fights inflammation. An article published in November of 2017 states that an anti-inflammatory diet is good for individuals with rheumatoid arthritis. The authors were specific that an anti-inflammatory diet may help slow down the disease, reduce the need for rheumatoid arthritis medication, and reduce joint damage.

IN MAY 2019, another prospective and small research revealed that when individuals with cancer of the rectum and colon adhere to an anti-inflammatory diet, there were reduced gastrointestinal issues reported by them, and the diet also increased their overall well-being.

ACCORDING to a September 2018 publication in the *Journal Of Internal Medicine,* adherence to an anti-inflammatory diet was connected to reduce cancer-induced death by thirteen percent; this study was carried out on almost seventy thousand Swedish adults to ensure accuracy. According to the authors, smokers who indulge in anti-inflammatory diets have their chance of death reduced by thirty percent. Although an anti-inflammatory diet is effective on smokers, it is counterproductive when you keep smoking. Yes, it will work but not as effective as it should.

Anti-Inflammatory Diet for Beginners   59

. . .

BELOW ARE *other ways that an anti-inflammatory diet can help (According to research)*

- Protection of the heart
- Managing pain associated with getting older
- Athletic training recovery
- Better quality of life for individuals with several sclerosis

List Of Foods To Eat On An Anti-Inflammatory Diet

An anti-inflammatory diet is basically stocking up on foods that have been proven by research to reduce inflammation. This means that you stay away from foods that spike inflammation or cause it. The best thing about the inflammatory diet is that it is rich in variety; this means that there are more than enough food choices to choose from. An anti-inflammatory diet is not like being a vegetarian or going vegan. You have to totally abstain from certain food types.

Anti-Inflammatory Foods

- **Plant-Based Proteins:** lentils, seitan, and chickpeas.
- **Fresh Fruit:** blueberries, apples, mangoes, pomegranates, tomatoes, grapefruit, grapes, blueberries, and peaches.
- **Vegetables:** Cauliflower, broccoli, bok choy, and brussels sprouts.
- **Whole Grains:** barley, whole-wheat bread, brown rice, and oatmeal.
- **Dried fruit:** plums

- **Fatty Fish:** sardines, herring, mackerel, lake trout, albacore tuna, and salmon.
- **Nuts:** Walnuts and almonds
- **Leafy Greens:** Romaine lettuce, kale, and spinach.
- **Seeds:** flaxseed and chia seeds
- **Ginger**
- **Red wine (not excessively)**
- **Coffee**
- **Omega-3 fatty acids:** olive oil and avocado oil
- **Dark chocolate (not excessively)**

NB: The foods mentioned after the colon are just examples as foods under each category are applicable.

Sample Of A One Week Anti-Inflammatory Diet

Anti-inflammatory foods have been elaborated on, and the foods that are needed have already been listed. Still, I have decided to add a one-week menu of an anti-inflammatory diet. This sample will help beginners create and master their own menu.

THE SAMPLE MAY NOT BE ideal for everyone, but it will certainly help people who do not want to subscribe to it draw inspiration to create theirs.

The First Day

Breakfast: blueberries and silvered almonds with steel-cut oats and coffee.

Lunch: Pomegranate seeds tossed with olive oil, beets, chickpeas with chopped kale salad, and lemon juice vinaigrette.

Dinner: A cauliflower crust embellished with salmon, anchovy, and tomato-topped pizza.

Snack: Unsalted raisins and nuts with homemade trail mix.

The Second Day

Breakfast: A cup of coffee with steel-cut oatmeal with sliced strawberries and walnut toppings

Lunch: Salmon sashimi with a side of ginger, brown rice, and broccoli

Dinner: A glass of red wine with kale, whitefish, barley, and ginger curry

Snack: Sliced mango

The Third Day

Breakfast: Blueberries and sliced banana with quinoa bowl, and almond butter accompanied with green tea

Lunch: Walnuts, grilled peaches, and albacore tuna with arugula salad

Dinner: A side of brown rice and grilled salmon with spinach salad

Snack: Grapes (frozen)

The Fourth Day

Breakfast: A cup of coffee, mushroom and kale frittata, and half a grapefruit

Lunch: Sauteed bok choy, brown rice, chick peas, with the grain bowl

Dinner: A side of smoked brussels sprouts with a veggie burger on a whole-grain bun

Snack: Unsalted mixed nuts

The Fifth Day

Breakfast: A cup of green tea, almond butter with chia seed pudding, and apple slices
   Lunch: Shredded carrots and tuna with spinach salad
   Dinner: A glass of red wine, red peppers stuffed with chickpeas, ground turkey, and quinoa
   Snack: Unsalted almonds

The Sixth Day

Breakfast: A cup of coffee and fresh blueberries with soy yogurt
   Lunch: Avocado, black beans, sardines, sauteed spinach, and tomatoes, all with a Quinoa bowl
   Dinner: a spinach salad and lentils with salmon
   Snack: Small handful of unsalted nuts and dark chocolate square.

The Seventh Day

Breakfast: A cup of coffee with peanut butter and banana sandwich
   Lunch: Halved cherry tomatoes on top of whole-grain toast and smashed avocado, and cottage cheese
   Dinner: Broccoli stir-fried in olive oil, mushroom, and seitan with bell peppers
   Snack: Cherries

Anti-Inflammatory Diet: Health Benefits

An anti-inflammatory diet has been proven to be good for individuals with cancer, epilepsy, diabetes, heart disease, Alzheimer's disease, and Pulmonary disease.

. . .

THE DOWNSIDES of an anti-inflammatory diet are few and far between, so it is an overall healthy diet and beneficial to individuals without inflammation. Adaptation might be an issue for some individuals when starting an anti-inflammatory diet, especially if you love dairy, processed foods, and meat; it may take a while to get used to the new eating style and habit. More time will have to be dedicated to cooking meals from scratch instead of consuming fast food.

Expected Differences When Anti-Inflammatory Diet IS Adopted

When individuals adopt an anti-inflammatory diet, they begin to feel better overall. All of the insanity that goes on in the body before the diet goes away. There will be a significant change in an individual's mood because when one feels better, one becomes happier.

AS FAR AS a health condition is concerned, immediate changes should not be expected. Changes in health conditions show in about two or three weeks, and it takes about two months to determine if the changes are long-lasting. This theory was propagated by the American Osteopathic Association's website.

THIS HAS BEEN MENTIONED a lot but having an anti-inflammatory diet is a great way to eating whether you have or do not have chronic inflammation. Most of the foods in an anti-inflammatory diet are needed for your overall well-being. Everyone stands to benefit from such a diet.

The Best Anti-Inflammatory Foods

An anti-inflammatory diet may be difficult for some to adapt to, while others crave it and only want the best. Some anti-inflammatory foods are more efficient than others. A list of the thirteen best anti-inflammatory foods to make up that diet has been compiled. The foods in this list can make up your anti-inflammatory diet menu, and they are all listed with their nutrients. Some of the foods listed have been mentioned above, but they are listed here with their nutrients.

- **Fatty Fish**

Fatty fish has a lot of protein and EPA, and DHA (long-chain omega-3 fatty acids). Basically, every type of fatty fish has omega-3 fatty acids, but the ones with the most amount include sardines, mackerel, salmon, anchovies, and herring.

Inflammation can lead to kidney disease, metabolic syndrome, and heart disease eradicated by DHA and EPA. These fatty acids are metabolized by your body into compounds known as protectins and resolvins; these compounds help to fight against inflammation.

According to research, people that consume supplements with EPA and DHA experienced a decrease in the inflammatory marker C-reactive protein (CRP). Another study also shows that individuals with irregular heartbeats who consumed EPA and DHA had no changes in inflammatory markers.

- **Avocados**

AVOCADOS ARE one of the most overlooked anti-inflammatory foods. They are stacked with heart-healthy monosaturated fats,

potassium, fiber, and magnesium. Avocados are rich in tocopherols and carotenoids, which can reduce the risk of cancer (which is usually the end result of severe inflammation).

Additionally, a compound in avocados has the probability of decreasing inflammation in young skin cells. This makes the food good for people with the probability of IBD, so if you have a family member with IBD, you should get an avocado right away.

According to a study, individuals who ate a hamburger with an avocado slice had reduced levels of inflammatory markers IL-6 and NF-kB. This result was compared with those of individuals who only consumed hamburgers.

- **Berries**

BERRIES ARE some of the smallest foods on this list, but their size does not deter them as they are packed with minerals, vitamins, and fiber. There is an endless list of berries, but the best for an anti-inflammatory diet are blueberries, blackberries, strawberries, and raspberries.

Berries are rich in antioxidants known as anthocyanins. Anthocyanins have anti-inflammatory effects that decrease heart disease risk. Natural killer cells (NK cells) are produced by the human body to ensure the proper function of your immune system.

According to a study in men, more NK cells were produced by men who ate blueberries daily instead of those who did not. Another study shows that overweight adults who consumed strawberries had reduced certain inflammatory markers that can cause heart disease.

- **Broccoli**

Like most vegetables, broccoli has excessive nutrients. Broccoli is a cruciferous vegetable just like kale, cauliflower, and brussels sprouts. According to research, enough consumption of cruciferous vegetables is linked to a reduced risk of cancer and heart disease. This is a possibility because cruciferous vegetables have antioxidants that fight inflammation.

Broccoli is rich in an antioxidant called sulforaphane. Sulforaphane battles inflammation via the reduction of NF-kB and cytokine levels.

- **Green Tea**

GREEN TEA HAS BEEN MENTIONED several times in this book, and it is no coincidence. Green tea is one of the healthiest beverages out there. It has so many functions like reducing the risk of obesity, cancer, heart disease, Alzheimer's disease, and many ailments.

Green tea has anti-inflammatory and antioxidant properties, which give it most of its benefits. A substance is known as epigallocatechin-3-gallate (EGCG) especially helps in the battle against inflammation.

Inflammation is reduced by EGCG by cutting down pro-inflammatory cytokine production and stops damage to your cells' fatty acids. Green tea is easily accessible and is available in online stores.

- **Grapes**

ANTHOCYANINS THAT REDUCE inflammation are found in grapes. The risks of many diseases like obesity, eye disorders, diabetes, and heart disease are reduced by grapes.

Resveratrol, a compound that is beneficial to an individual's overall well-being, is also found in grapes. According to a study, individuals with heart disease who engaged in daily consumption of grapes experienced reduced inflammatory gene markers. These individuals also experienced increased levels of adiponectin; reduced levels of adiponectin are linked with weight gain and heightens the risk of cancer.

- **Peppers**

CHILI AND BELL peppers have many antioxidants and vitamin C that helps in the fight against inflammation. Chili peppers have ferulic and sinapic acid that helps in the reduction of inflammation and ensure a healthy aging process.

Quercetin is an antioxidant provided by bell peppers that helps in the reduction of one marker of oxidative damage in individuals with sarcoidosis. Sarcoidosis is a disease caused by inflammation.

- **Turmeric**

TURMERIC IS QUITE nutritious and has a lot of health benefits. It has a sturdy and earthy flavor that is used regularly in Indian dishes and curries.

Turmeric is mostly preferred in the fight against inflammation because it has high curcumin. This powerful nutrient helps in the fight against inflammation. Inflammation related to diabetes, arthritis, and other conditions is lowered by turmeric.

In research, daily consumption of 1 gram of curcumin and piperine (from black pepper) resulted in a notable reduction in inflammatory marker C-reactive protein in individuals with

metabolic syndrome. However, it might be difficult to attain the required amount of curcumin to get the needed effect from turmeric alone.

According to research, overweight women who had a daily consumption of turmeric (2.8 grams) displayed no signs of improved inflammatory markers. It is better to take supplements with isolated curcumin. Curcumin absorption can be boosted by two thousand percent by a combination of curcumin supplements and piperine. Turmeric is available in many online stores and actual grocery shops.

- **Mushrooms**

There is a plethora of mushrooms worldwide, but only a handful are commercially grown and edible. Edible mushrooms include shiitake, truffles, and portobello mushrooms. Mushrooms are rich in selenium, B vitamins, and copper. Mushrooms have phenols and other antioxidants that help in the battle against inflammation.

Obesity-related and low-grade inflammation can be reduced by *lion's mane,* a special type of mushroom. However, mushrooms are only effective against inflammation when they are lightly cooked or consumed raw; consuming them after proper cooking significantly reduces their anti-inflammatory compounds.

- **Cherries**

Cherries have antioxidants like catechins and anthocyanins that help in the battle against inflammation. Oh, and they are really delicious, which makes them a great substitute for sweetened foods.

Researchers have spent more time checking the health

benefits of tart cherries than other cherry types, but sweet cherries are also beneficial. According to research, individuals who consumed 280 grams of cherry daily consecutively for thirty days experienced a decrease in their inflammatory marker levels (CRP). The markers even remained in a reduced state a month after the individuals have stopped cherry consumption.

- **Extra Virgin Olive Oil**

One of the healthiest foods any individual can consume is extra virgin olive oil. It is a staple in the extremely healthy Mediterranean diet and has many monounsaturated fats.

According to research, extra virgin olive oil has reduced the risk of brain cancer, heart disease, and other near-fatal ailments. According to a study on the *Mediterranean diet, individuals who consumed 1.7 ounces (50 ml) of olive oil experienced a reduction in CRP and other inflammatory markers every day.*

Anti-inflammatory drugs like ibuprofen have similar effects with oleocanthal (olive oil antioxidant); this makes extra virgin olive oil a better option to fight inflammation as opposed to ibuprofen. The anti-inflammatory benefits of extra virgin olive oil supersede the ones found in more refined olive oils because extra virgin olive oil is mostly made from natural extracts.

Extra virgin olive oil can be purchased in any local grocery store, but it is also available online.

- **Cocoa And Dark Chocolate**

DARK CHOCOLATE IS by far the most delicious food on this list; it is quite satisfying. Apart from the excitement it brings to the taste buds, dark chocolate is inflammation-reducing antioxidants. The antioxidants lower the risk of disease and help with

the aging process by making it healthy; simply put, "dark chocolate makes you age with grace."

The anti-inflammatory effects of chocolates are aided by flavanols. Flavanols also ensure that the endothelial cells that line your arteries stay healthy. According to a study, there was a significant improvement in endothelial function experienced by smokers who ate chocolates with high flavanol content. This improvement was experienced within two hours.

However, ensure to opt for dark chocolate that has seventy percent of cocoa content. If you can have more than seventy percent cocoa, it is even better. This is to ensure the anti-inflammatory benefits of dark chocolate are fully experienced.

Like most of the foods in this list, dark chocolate can be found in your local grocery store, but it can also be gotten online.

- **Tomatoes**

TOMATOES HAVE BEEN SAVED for last because of their flexibility. It can be consumed in different ways, making its benefits endless. Tomatoes are high in potassium, vitamin C, and lycopene, all of which help in the fight against inflammation.

Lycopene is especially functional in the reduction of inflammatory compounds that cause different cancer types. According to a study, consumption of tomato juice caused a significant reduction of inflammatory markers in overweight women. You can cook tomatoes in olive oil to fully maximize the lycopene amount absorbed because lycopene is a nutrient called carotenoid. It is best absorbed with a source of fat.

The lowest inflammation levels can always lead to disease if not properly managed. Ensure inflammation is properly managed by opting for different foods with antioxidants. Dark

chocolate, extra virgin olive oil, fish, and peppers are among the strongest foods that help in the battle against inflammation. The foods in this list will guide you as you prepare your anti-inflammatory diet and begin your journey to overall healthy life.

6

CHAPTER SIX: THE LIFELONG BENEFITS OF ANTI-INFLAMMATORY DIET

The first purpose of an anti-inflammatory diet is quite obvious. It reduces the risk of inflammatory diseases and lowers the chance of inflammation. However, there are several lifelong benefits that an anti-inflammatory diet gives to individuals whether they are battling inflammation or not. Some of these benefits include;

- **Improved Fertility**

Most individuals are unaware that inflammation plays a role in infertility in both males and females. This means that infertility is highest when there is no inflammation or when it is low. The risk of miscarriage and pre-eclampsia is lowered when inflammation is reduced and/or avoided during pregnancy. Omega-3 fish oils and antioxidants are great for the improvement of fertility and eradicate possible pregnancy complications.

For the benefit of those unaware, *pre-eclampsia* is a condition where a pregnant woman experiences high blood pressure putting the mother and child in danger. According to a study in

2018, pre-eclampsia is linked to pro-inflammatory cytokines. This study was carried out at the University Of Mississippi Medical Center. The risk of pre-eclampsia in pregnancy is reduced by an anti-inflammatory diet via the regulation of cytokines.

- **Lowered Risk Of Autoimmune Disorders**

AUTOIMMUNE DISORDERS and inflammation have happened so often together that they can be interchanged at this point. Some autoimmune disorders cause inflammation, while in other cases, autoimmune disorders are caused by inflammation. When autoimmunity is triggered in the body, the immune system destroys healthy tissue by going into hyper attack mode. Ailments caused by autoimmune disorders include lupus, grave's disease, rheumatoid arthritis, celiac disease, multiple sclerosis, and Addison's disease.

It is only logical that developing the disorders, as mentioned earlier, is decreased by the reduced risk of inflammation. That sounds like a mouthful, but it is the way it should be. Identifying and tackling a diet that causes inflammation via autoimmune response can ensure that inflammation does not occur.

- **Lowers Risk Of Cancer And Can Help To Fight It**

THERE HAS BEEN a plethora of research with evidence that foods like fruits, vegetables, and whole grains help reduce the risk of cancer and help in the battle against it. However, such foods will only be effective when foods like bad fats and red meat are avoided.

When inflammation occurs, the sick or damaged cells go

through a state of chaos, which is especially predominant in cancer cells. Inflammation provides a "healing ground" for the diseased cells instead of attacking and terminating them. This "healing ground" does not just allow them to recover; it allows them to multiply. Inflammation can be kept in check with a proper anti-inflammatory diet.

- **Strong Bones**

MOST FOODS in an anti-inflammatory diet contain bone-strengthening foods. However, not all foods have that, but if those specific foods form most of the anti-inflammatory diet, your bone strength will be off the charts. Anti-inflammatory foods like these prevent thinning of the bone tissue called osteoporosis.

If you want strong bones, look for anti-inflammatory foods that have strong phytonutrients' concentration. Phytonutrients are plant-based antioxidants that go head-to-head with the free radicals responsible for several ailments like osteoporosis. Lycopene and beta-carotene are examples of phytonutrients.

- **Reduced Diabetes And Metabolic Syndrome Risk**

There is an association between insulin resistance and high insulin levels with a reduced ability for glucose to be taken by cells. These are precursors and signs of diabetes known as prediabetes. The entire process is worsened by inflammation caused by high levels of insulin. High glucose and high insulin reduce the responsiveness of the cells. The risk of developing glucose dysregulation and insulin resistance is increased by inflammation.

According to a study in 2019, researchers concluded that the connection between type 1 and type 2 diabetes and inflamma-

tion is strong enough that more research into this connection is required to help tackle the prevalence of diabetes.

- **Reduced Cholesterol Levels**

Cardiovascular disease is not always caused by high cholesterol levels. Still, it should never be overlooked as it heightens the risk. Adaptation of an anti-inflammatory lifestyle and diet can reduce your cholesterol because foods that heighten triglyceride and blood cholesterol levels are removed from your diet; this means that anti-inflammatory foods do not have high cholesterol. In case you are wondering about the connection between cholesterol levels and inflammation, it is important to know that inflammatory foods also increase triglyceride and blood cholesterol levels. Avoid foods like cured meats, inflammatory protein sources, and fried foods. Foods like fruits, whole grains, vegetables, and legumes should be eaten to fight inflammation and reduced cholesterol levels.

According to research, the reduction of inflammation reduces the chances of cardiovascular disease. The methods these foods utilize to reduce inflammation and cholesterol level are different, just like the foods. Some foods provide soluble fiber that helps the body get rid of cholesterol before destroying any important ligament in the body. Other foods contain substances from plants, and some perform this reduction by reducing the LDL.

- **Sharp Brain**

The inflammation signal C-reactive protein (hsCRP) is confirmed by many experts to play a role in cardiovascular, and heart disease interferes with cognitive function in humans. It has also been confirmed to have a connection to Alzheimer's disease.

One does not have to be diagnosed with any inflammatory disease to start an anti-inflammatory diet. An anti-inflammatory diet can be followed at a very tender age. According to a study in 2018, a group of 800 Australian teens that consume sweets, red meats, and processed foods has a high chance of ending up mentally ill or obese. The teens who use an anti-inflammatory diet had no signs of mental illness or obesity. This research was published in the journal *Brain, Behavior, and Immunity*.

The mental benefits the anti-inflammatory diet gives you continue as you get older. According to 2019 research, an anti-inflammatory diet does not just safeguard the brain; it significantly prohibits neuroinflammation that can cause Alzheimer's disease.

- **Lose Weight**

Inflammatory foods can lead to weight gain. An anti-inflammatory diet will enhance reasonable weight loss. Your fat cells accumulate toxins, making it difficult for the cells to provide chemical signals to the other part of your body that handles endocrine function and metabolism. Inflammation reduction ensures that all your cells have the right coating of membrane and ensure overall well-being.

Weight stabilization is enhanced by the chemical signals and ensures your bodily function is at its best. Weight and hormones are regulated by the endocrine system, the risk of diabetes, metabolic syndrome, and several others are influenced by the endocrine system. The endocrine system begins to malfunction when toxins are stacked up in fat cells.

Inflammation and obesity are always side by side as inflammation enhances the latter. According to research in 2013, obesity is heavily promoted by inflammation. However, weight loss facilitated by an anti-inflammatory diet with several nutri-

Anti-Inflammatory Diet for Beginners   77

ents and vitamins, inflammatory risk factors can be lowered, and the risk of chronic diseases will be significantly reduced.

- **Reduced Risk Of Cardiovascular And Heart Disease**

High cholesterol levels have taken the blame for causing heart disease for so long, but inflammation is the major cause. Cholesterol is just a reaction of the body to the damage inflicted by inflammation.

The amount of inflammatory substance produced by your body is measured by a blood test known as the highly sensitive cardio C-reactive protein (hsCRP). When hsCRP is elevated in an individual, the risk of heart disease can be lowered by anti-inflammation.

- **Better Mood**

Inflammation is the body's natural way of healing. Still, when it is elongated, then that is a problem and causes discomfort in individuals. Individuals begin to experience pains in the arms and legs, tiredness, sleeplessness, and a heightened risk of heart disease or cancer. Anyone going through all of this will certainly be in a nasty mood. However, when inflammation is reduced via an anti-inflammatory diet, all the pains and discomfort go away, which puts individuals in a better mood.

7

CONCLUSION

At this point, you know all there is to know about inflammation and the numerous complications it can cause if not properly managed. An anti-inflammatory diet is the best way to tackle inflammation; the diet given in this book contains the best anti-inflammatory foods; these foods have been tested and proven to be effective.

Printed in Great Britain
by Amazon

76809381R00047

But all Sam could think of was that Obby was in trouble. They would have to go back. That much was certain.

"But he's my friend! We can't just leave him!"
Sam stamped her foot and burst into tears.
"We'll think of something," promised Ben.
"We like Obby too, Sam. But we need to talk
about this. Come on, cheer up."

"I didn't like that," said Mouse. He looked pale.

"Nor did I," agreed Jojo, shakily.

"We shouldn't have left him," said Sam. "He's in trouble, I just know it."

"So would we be, if we hadn't escaped," said Ben.

The crashing sounds were coming closer.

The children looked at each other and ran for the lift. Obby reached in with his paw and hit the button. As the doors closed, the last thing they saw was his funny, furry face peering at them.

Chapter Two

A Narrow Escape

Obby clapped his paws together. With a great grinding sound, the cave wall cracked in two – and there stood the lift, with its doors open!
"But what about you?" shouted Sam.
"Never mind me! Get in the lift! Now, while there's still time!"

"What's the matter?" asked Sam.

"Sssh! Listen!"

Everyone listened. There were distant crashing noises coming from outside. In the background, they could hear the roll of distant thunder. Suddenly, the cave seemed to get much darker.

"Go!" shouted Obby. "Go, quickly! You're in great danger!"

Obby scuttled to the door and pulled it shut.
"Gong," he said. His furry face was grim.
"Gone?" said Ben. "Who's gone?"
"Not gone, silly boy, Gong! Giant Gong.
Great big bully. Spoils everything. Thinks he can
do what he likes. But he doesn't scare me. I've put
up posters, I have. All over the woods.
Down With Gong, they say …"
Suddenly, he broke off.

"That was the best soup I've ever had," said Ben, scraping his bowl clean. "You're a great cook."
"Really?" said Obby, sounding pleased. "Well, you're doing me a favour, coming to call. Don't get many visitors these days. Because of *You Know Who*. I'm not afraid to stand up to him, though."
"Who?" asked Mouse.

"How do you do it, Obby?" asked Sam, with her mouth full. "Is it magic?"

"Of course," said Obby, with a little chuckle. "Magic Toadstools, see? Soup tastes however you want it to. Old family recipe. Want some more?

"Yes, please!" said everyone.

He picked up his spoon and took a tiny sip.

"You're all wrong," he said. "It's toffee fudge. I love toffee fudge!"

Jojo tried a spoonful. "Banana milkshake," she said, firmly. "Go on, Mouse. It's delicious."

Mouse looked down at his bowl. Should he? It looked so nasty. But the others were busily tucking in.

Much to their surprise, a big grin spread over Ben's face.
"It's lovely," he said.
"Like chocolate ice cream. But hot. Try it."

Sam took a sip.
"No," she said.
"Jam rolypoly with custard. My favourite!"

He lifted his spoon and took a tiny sip.
The others waited, eyes on stalks.

"Well?" they said.

"Nonsense," said Obby. "Been slaving over a hot stove all morning. I'll get very obbygobulous if you don't eat it."

"That means he stamps and shouts," whispered Sam, with a giggle.

"You're quite sure it's safe?" asked Ben.

"Trust me," said Obby.

"Here goes, then," said Ben.

Obby plonked the pot down and began to ladle thick, green liquid into the bowls.

"Eat!" he commanded.

The children stared down at their bowls, then at each other. "Er ... we're not that hungry," said Jojo. "We've just had breakfast."

"Er – what is it?" asked Mouse.

"What do you think? Toadstool Soup, of course. That's all we Obbygobulums eat. Except on Fridays, when we have fish."

The children looked at each other. Ben took a deep breath. "But surely toadstools are poisonous," he said.

"Not these. They're special."

"What a lovely cave!" said Jojo.

"Think so?" said Obby. "Well, it's small, but it suits me. You'll have to sit on the floor. Only the one chair, see. Right. Grub's up."

Inside, the cave was warm and cosy. Portraits of cross looking Obbygobulums hung on the walls. There was a table, set with four bowls and spoons. There was a tiny bed, a rickety little wardrobe and a wooden chair.

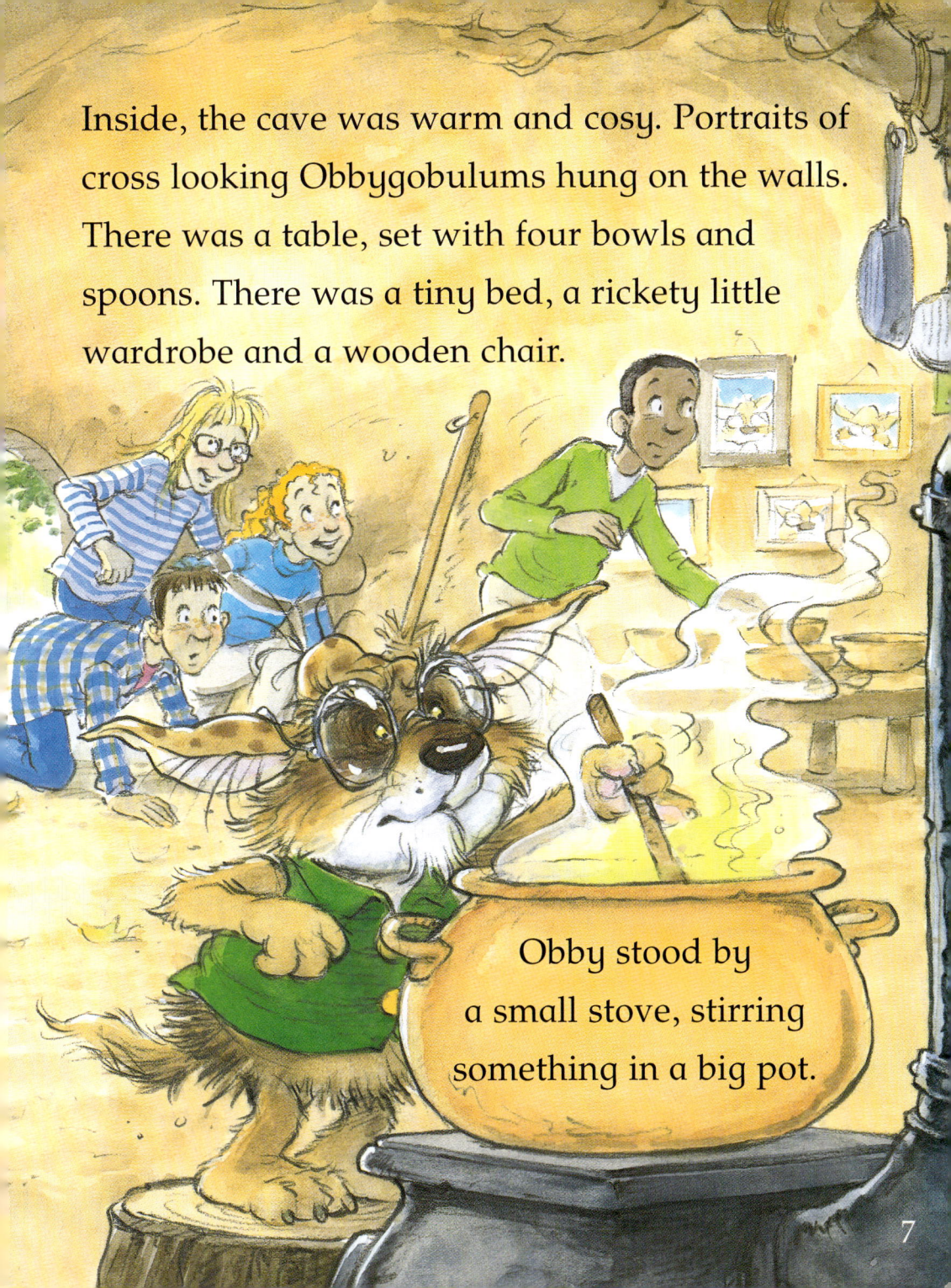

Obby stood by a small stove, stirring something in a big pot.

"He's rather grumpy, isn't he?" whispered Mouse.
"That's part of his charm," said Sam.
They had to bend low to go through the little door.

"I brought my friends," said Sam. "Ben, Jojo, and Mouse."

"Hello, Obby," said Ben, Jojo and Mouse.

"Hello yourself," said Obby. "Are you coming in or not?"

And he bobbed back in again.

The door opened, and out poked Obby's head. His huge glasses were all steamed up. In his paw, he held a big wooden spoon.

"There you are!" he snapped. "About time. Soup's been ready for ages."

The doors slid back and everyone stepped out into a leafy glade. Birds were singing. Sunshine speckled the leaves. Nearby, was a small river with a raft tied to a tree. Ahead, was a little green door set into a rock face.

Chapter One
Back to Beyond

In the lift, three pairs of eyes stared at Sam.

"You met a what?" asked Ben.

"An Obbygobulum," said Sam. "I couldn't sleep, so I came to the lift and pushed the magic button. But instead of Strange Street, I ended up in the Wild Woods. That's where I met Obby."

"What's an Obbygobulum?" asked Jojo.

"You'll see," chuckled Sam. And she pushed the button.

Soup with Obby

written by Kaye Umansky
illustrated by Steve Smallman